The Delaplaine

2018 Long Weekend Guide

Andrew Delaplaine

NO BUSINESS HAS PAID A SINGLE PENNY OR GIVEN _ANYTHING_ TO BE INCLUDED IN THIS BOOK.

A list of the author's other travel guides, as well as his political thrillers and titles for children, can be found at the end of this book.

Contributors
James Cubby

Gramercy Park Press
New York – London - Paris

Please submit corrections, additions or comments to
andrewdelaplaine@mac.com

ATLANTA
The Delaplaine
2018 Long Weekend Guide

TABLE OF CONTENTS

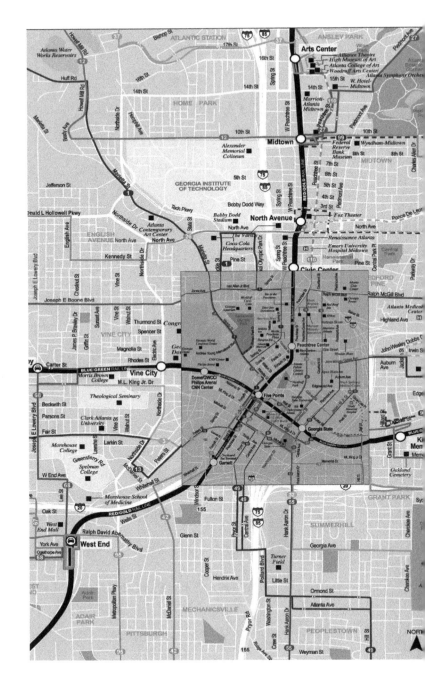

Chapter 1
WHY ATLANTA?

Hotlanta?

There's no city that can lay a greater claim to represent what used to be termed the "New South" than the city of Atlanta.

It was burned down in the Civil War (or as my Fifth Grade teacher Mrs. McCutcheon sternly reminded me in the 1960s, "the War of Northern Aggression") during General Sherman's famous "March to the Sea," and to this day remains the only major American city completely annihilated by war. Sherman burned all the railroad depots, uprooted the tracks, burned every business to the ground and for good measure to show that he meant it, burned down two-thirds of the private homes.

Perhaps that's why Atlanta's resurgence so captured the imagination. When it became the home of the Civil Rights Movement in the 1960s, led by Dr. Martin Luther King, Jr., Atlanta took on yet another level of symbolic importance.

Non-natives are familiar if not with Atlanta itself, then surely with its huge airport. Hartsfield-Jackson International Airport is the world's busiest airport, with more than 88 million annual passengers. (By comparison, London's Heathrow only has 64 million people passing through it.)

Hosting the Olympics in 1996 gave Atlanta an international profile and drove many upgrades to the city. The **MARTA** public transport system is efficient and a major addition to the city's infrastructure. **Underground Atlanta** has added to the nightlife sector. The **World Congress Center** was built to attract the most desirable convention business and it has worked.

It's "Hotlanta" all right.

Chapter 2
GETTING ABOUT

Atlanta is unique in that it has 3 separate skylines. Downtown, Midtown and Buckhead each has its own skyline that would make an admirable statement by itself.

DOWNTOWN consists of **Five Points**, **Centennial Park**, Sweet Auburn, Castleberry Hill and the **Hotel District**. This is where you'll find the state Capitol, City Hall, the **CNN Center**, **Georgia Aquarium** and the **World of Coca-Cola Museum**. While most tourists congregate in Downtown, I advise you not to make the same mistake. Locals tend to disappear from Downtown after dark, so you should follow them to one of the many completely different neighborhoods they go to at night.

MIDTOWN is the area just north of Downtown. It's a major business and residential district with big buildings and a concentrated nightlife section. Piedmont Park, the Woodruff Arts Center and the Georgia Tech campus are located here.

BUCKHEAD is a few miles north of Midtown. It's a popular business and nightlife area. Buckhead is surrounded by neighboring **Brookwood Hills**, as well as Peachtree Battle, **Lindbergh Center**, and the Governor's Mansion.

EAST ATLANTA, also called **East Atlanta Village,** has great neighborhoods with beautiful homes, some of the best bars and restaurants in town and a bustling shopping scene. It's a gentrifying area, but it's cool. It's south of I-20 and Moreland Avenue.

INMAN PARK, LITTLE FIVE POINTS, CANDLER PARK are clustered together and are a center for nightlife and no-hype restaurants favored by the locals. Little Five Points has great murals you'll see as you walk around.

VIRGINIA-HIGHLANDS is nearby—it has some of the nicer housing in the area.

BY CAR

As anyone who's been here knows, downtown traffic in Atlanta is a nightmare at rush hour. If you're only on a short visit, forego getting a rental car and rely on cabs or MARTA to get around.

BY FOOT

Once you're in any given neighborhood, walking is just fine. Shops, restaurants and bars are usually clustered together, so whether you're in Inman Park, Little Five Points, Midtown, Downtown, etc., you'll be OK. It's getting between these little neighborhoods that presents a challenge. This is where you'll want to grab a taxi or use MARTA.

MARTA

The Metropolitan Atlanta Rapid Transit Authority, www.itsmarta.com, runs the trains and bus lines and does a very good job. (Various passes, called **Breeze Cards**, are available, depending on how long you're in town.)

TAXI

In dense areas like Downtown, cabs are easy to get. But you can always call ahead: Checker Cab: 404-351-1111. www.atlantacheckercab.com

Chapter 3
WHERE TO STAY

ARTMORE HOTEL
1302 West Peachtree St, NW, 404-876-6100
www.artmorehotel.com
NEIGHBORHOOD: Midtown
This unique Midtown boutique hotel delivers personalized service. Once you get past the inauspicious façade, you'll discover an historic landmark dating from 1924 that has

been restored beautifully. It was an old apartment building that still has lovely Spanish design themes and an offbeat charm. In good weather, you can join the other guests as they sip cocktails around a fountain that also has a fire pit. Has several split-level suites. Located across the street from MARTA, High Museum, Alliance Theater and the Atlanta Symphony Orchestra. This is a fine option if you don't want to stay in one of the big chain hotels.

THE ELLIS
176 Peachtree St. NW, 404-523-5155
www.ellishotel.com
NEIGHBORHOOD: Downtown
Charming Downtown property in a building dating back to 1913. It was reopened in 2007 after a thorough renovation costing over $25 million. Nothing fusty about it; completely modern and sleek. Bamboo paneling in the rooms and limestone in the baths. The **Terrace Bistro** makes a good spot for people-watching as you overlook Peachtree Street. (It also has very good food from local farms.)

FOUR SEASONS

75 14th St. NE, 404-881-9898

www.fourseasons.com/atlanta/

NEIGHBORHOOD: Midtown

Offering typical Four Seasons luxurious accommodations and service. This location boasts 244 ultra-spacious guest rooms including 18 luxury suites. Amenities available: spa treatments, indoor saline lap pool, and Atlanta's most luxurious fitness center.

GEORGIAN TERRACE

659 Peachtree St NE, 404-897-1991

thegeorgianterrace.com

NEIGHBORHOOD: Midtown, Business & Cultural District

This gorgeous old 326-room Beaux Arts hotel (dating from 1911) was the site of the premiere gala for *Gone With the Wind* in 1939. Listed on the National

Register of Historic Places, this hotel is known for its dramatic vistas and excellent Southern service. Located just a few steps from the historic Fox Theatre, where "Gone With the Wind" premiered. Clark Gable actually stayed here. If you're not staying here, at least stop in to enjoy a drink at the elegant high-ceilinged bar with its charming crown molding. Amenities include a rooftop pool, a friendly bar, and a sexy speakeasy in the basement. Some of their rooms are part of the "Southern Living Hotel Collection," a list of 4 and 5-star independent resorts carefully vetted and approved by "Southern Living" magazine.

HIGHLAND INN

644 North Highland Ave., 404-874-5756
www.thehighlandinn.com/
NEIGHBORHOOD: Poncey/Highland
Historic hotel, built in 1927, with great service. Basic but comfortable accommodations and surprisingly affordable. Great location.

HOTEL INDIGO
683 Peachtree St. NE, 404-874-9200
www.hotelindigo.com
NEIGHBORHOOD: Midtown
What used to be an old Days Inn has been beautifully transformed into a chic boutique hotel property. (About a mile north of the Aquarium.)

MANDARIN ORIENTAL
3376 Peachtree Rd. NE, 404-995-7500
www.mandarinoriental.com/atlanta
NEIGHBORHOOD: Buckhead
Five-star luxury hotel features beautiful rooms, superb restaurant and an elegant spa. Offering 117 luxurious rooms with large bathrooms and 10 spacious suites with balconies. Located close to the Atlanta Botanical Garden, Georgia Aquarium and the High Museum of Art.

MICROTEL INN & SUITES
1840 Corporate Blvd., 404-325-4446
www.microtelinn.com
NEIGHBORHOOD: Buckhead
Out in Buckhead, this is a super choice for families. This budget property has a microwave in the room, a refrigerator and free Continental breakfast.

RITZ-CARLTON - BUCKHEAD
3434 Peachtree Rd. NE, 404-237-2700
www.ritzcarlton.com
NEIGHBORHOOD: Buckhead
This property offers the hospitality and sophistication that one would expect from a Ritz-Carlton. This location has 510 elegantly appointed guest rooms including 56 suites featuring bay window views of the city's skyline.

Ritz-Carlton boasts intimate service and luxurious accommodations, an exclusive **Spa**, exquisite dining.

RITZ-CARLTON
181 Peachtree St. NE, 404-659-0400
www.ritzcarlton.com
NEIGHBORHOOD: Downtown
This Ritz-Carlton is located in the heart of Atlanta and features beautiful interiors. This location has 444 elegantly appointed rooms, including 22 suites with bay window views of the downtown Atlanta skyline. Amenities include: luxury hotel lobby bar, Wireless High-Speed Internet Access (daily fee applies), and iPod docking stations.

ST. REGIS
88 W. Paces Ferry Rd., 404-563-7900
www.stregisatlanta.com/
NEIGHBORHOOD: Buckhead
The St. Regis has a great environment that is a must see. It's the tops for luxury and grandeur with its majestic staircases, crystal chandeliers. It's got a little bit of

everything: great hotel service (Egyptian cotton sheets on the beds, marble baths), a wine bar, **Astor Court**, afternoon tea, and a great bar modeled after the famous King Cole Bar in New York's St. Regis. Only the mural behind the bar here is not of King Cole, but of a phoenix rising from the ashes, which is a motif extensively displayed in Atlanta. If you order the "Southern" cocktail, you'll be getting their bespoke bourbon made for the hotel by Woodford Reserve. The next-day suit service is handled by the famous local menswear designer, Sid Mashburn. Since Atlanta is the center of a booming film industry thanks to the state's attractive tax incentive program that lures Hollywood productions to Georgia, this place is a hotbed of celebrities.

STONEHURST PLACE B&B
923 Piedmont Ave. NE, 404-881-0722
www.stonehurstplace.com
NEIGHBORHOOD: Midtown
Built in 1896, this is Atlanta's only eco-friendly, luxury Bed & Breakfast with an excellent view of Piedmont Park (what Central Park is to Manhattan, Piedmont is

to Altnata). A beautiful B&B featuring only 6 lovely renovated rooms in a variety of sizes, some with queen beds, vintage baths and fireplaces, others with king beds, marble floors, spa tubs, and walk-in showers. Attentive service. You can walk through the garden where you'll find many of the plants labeled. Something I like to do at twilight is to sit on the front porch and watch the city lights come on. Amenities include: gourmet breakfast, hand-ironed luxury linens, iPod docking stations, wireless Internet and on-site parking. Non-smoking venue.

W ATLANTA
45 Ivan Allen Jr. Blvd., 404-582-5800
www.watlantadowntown.com
NEIGHBORHOOD: Downtown
The lush W Atlanta offers a convenient location near Atlanta nightlife and attractions like the Georgia Aquarium, Centennial Olympic Park and the Georgia Dome. Amenities include: cozy Living Room bar, outdoor heated pool, state-of-the-art fitness center, Bliss Spa and private heliport.

W ATLANTA
3377 Peachtree Rd. NE, 678-500-3100
www.watlantabuckhead.com
NEIGHBORHOOD: Buckhead
W Atlanta, an upscale boutique hotel, offers a prime
location near shopping, fine dining and entertainment.
Buckhead's hippest rooftop bar, Whiskey Blue Atlanta,
is located on the 12th floor. On site restaurant, Cook Hall,
offers contemporary cuisine. Other amenities include:
fully equipped fitness center, WET deck, and infinity-edge
pool overlooking Peachtree Road. Luxurious rooms come
with the latest technology like Wi-Fi.

WESTIN PEACHTREE PLAZA

210 Peachtree St. NW, 404-659-1400

www.westinpeachtreeplazaatlanta.com

NEIGHBORHOOD:

One of Atlanta's skyline icons, the revolving Sun Dial Restaurant tops off this 73-story hotel. Located downtown near all the attractions and attached to AmericasMart. 1,068 rooms featuring floor-to-ceiling windows, the Westin Heavenly Bed, marble Heavenly Bath, and cutting-edge entertainment.

Chapter 4
WHERE TO EAT

In "The Virginia House-Wife" by Mary Randolph, published in 1824, you'll find the first recipe for Southern Fried Chicken:

"Cut [the chicken] up as for the fricassee, dredge the pieces well with flour, sprinkle them with salt, put them into a good quantity of boiling lard, and fry them a light brown."

Can't get much simpler than that.

And yet such simplicity has allowed the term "fried chicken" to be interpreted in hundreds of thousands of different ways, almost all of them perfectly wonderful, to my mind, having been raised in South Carolina on a plantation.

With slaves adding spices redolent of their West African homeland, the variations on the theme exploded, and continue to unfold today.

Even in the finest of fine restaurants, you'll find world-renowned chefs unable to shake the urge to put their signature touch to this most American of all-American foods.

ALMA COCINA
191 Peachtree Street NE, 404-968-9662
www.alma-atlanta.com
CUISINE: Latin American, Brazilian, Mexican
DRINKS: Full Bar
SERVING: Lunch, Dinner
PRICE RANGE: $$
NEIGHBOROOD: Downtown
Serving up contemporary Latin and Mexican cuisine mixing fresh ingredients and traditional regional influences. Delicious menu selections like "Fried Avocado" tacos and "Chicken Mole Oaxaca." They have interesting twists on classic recipes. The Fried Avocado tacos, for instance, are served with a poblano pesto instead of salsa. They go to great lengths to make sure everything here is as good as it can possibly be. They even go down to Mexico to buy their tequila by the keg. Innovative cocktails.

ATKINS PARK RESTAURANT
794 N Highland Ave. NE, 404-876-7249
www.atkinspark.com
CUISINE: American (Traditional)
DRINKS: Full Bar
SERVING: Lunch, Dinner, Brunch
PRICE RANGE: $$

NEIGHBORHOOD: Virginia Highlands
Atlanta's oldest restaurant and bar located in the historical Atkins Park Tavern. This is a great dining spot for families. Great food and atmosphere.

ATLANTC SEAFOOD COMPANY
2345 Mansell Rd, Alpharetta, 770-640-0488
www.atlanticseafoodco.com/
CUISINE: Seafood/Sushi
DRINKS: Full Bar
SERVING: Lunch & Dinner during the week, Dinner on weekends
PRICE RANGE: $$$
NEIGHBORHOOD: Alpharetta
Modern eatery featuring a sushi bar. Menu includes favorites like crab cakes, lobster and the Soy-honey Chilean Sea bass. Great desserts.

ANTICO PIZZA
1093 Hemphill Ave NW, 404-724-2333
www.littleitalia.com
CUISINE: Pizza
DRINKS: No Booze
SERVING: Lunch, Dinner
PRICE RANGE: $$
NEIGHBOROOD: Westside/Home Park
Great pizza, some say the best in Atlanta. This
Neapolitan-style pizzeria is not only a local's favorite
but its pizzas have been ranked among the top five in the
country. Usually crowded but worth the wait.

B'S CRACKLIN'
2061 Main St NW, 470-765-6966
www.bscracklinbbq.com
CUISINE: Barbeque/Southern
DRINKS: Beer/Wine
SERVING: Lunch, Dinner
PRICE RANGE: $$
NEIGHBORHOOD: Riverside
Comfortable BBQ eatery offers Southern favorites like
Heritage-breed pork, brisket, chicken, and delicious sides.
Favorites: Cornbread and BBQ Ribs. Also, don't overlook
the pulled pork plate with coleslaw and okra. Inside and
outdoor seating. Local brewery beers.

BACCHANALIA

1198 Howell Mill Rd., 404-365-0410 ext 22

www.starprovisions.com

CUISINE: American

DRINKS: Full Bar

SERVING: Dinner

PRICE RANGE: $$$$

NEIGHBORHOOD: West Midtown

One of Atlanta's most celebrated restaurants serving great food with a fabulous wait staff and excellent wine selection. Chefs Quatrano and Clifford Harrison offer a seasonal menu with many items coming from their farm. Way back in 1993 when they opened, they were among the first to bring the farm-to-table philosophy to Atlanta. Lucky for them, they had a farm! A lot of chefs with their own celebrated eateries in Atlanta started off in the kitchen here, so that tells you how important this place is in the firmament of Atlanta culinary traditions.

BANTAM + BIDDY

1544 Piedmont Ave, 404-907-3469

www.bantamandbiddy.com

CUISINE: American (New); Diner

DRINKS: Full Bar

SERVING: Lunch, Dinner, Brunch

PRICE RANGE: $$

NEIGHBORHOOD: in town

Located in Ansley Mall, Bantam + Biddy offers a casual, family-friendly setting featuring regional, all-natural and pastured poultry. Get the crispy skin rotisserie bird served with different sauces.

BARCELONA

240 N. Highland Ave. NE, 404-589-1010

www.barcelonawinebar.com/

CUISINE: American; Spanish
DRINKS: Full Bar
SERVING: lunch / dinner
PRICE RANGE: $$$
NEIGHBORHOOD: Inman Park, 2 miles east of Downtown

Great wine selection and food. Spanish tapas and large plates: crispy cabbage, grilled hangar steak, chorizo with sweet & sour figs. Beautiful patio seating. Watering hole for many celebrities, Walking Dead, Vampire Diaries, to name a few.

BONES

3130 Piedmont Rd. NE, 404-237-2663

www.bonesrestaurant.com

CUISINE: Steakhouse
DRINKS: Full Bar
SERVING: Lunch, Dinner
PRICE RANGE: $$$$
NEIGHBORHOOD: Buckhead

Recognized as the best steakhouse in Atlanta (don't

tell Kevin Rathbun), serving prime beef, fresh seafood, and Maine lobster along with Southern regional specialties. Great service.

BRICK STORE PUB
125 E Court Square, Decatur, 404-687-0990
www.brickstorepub.com
CUISINE: American
DRINKS: Full Bar
SERVING: Lunch & Dinner
PRICE RANGE: $$
NEIGHBORHOOD: Decatur
Casual eatery with a menu of pub grub and great selection of beers. Menu favorites include: Cast iron pot pie and Fish 'n' chips.

BUSY BEE CAFÉ

810 Martin Luther King Jr Dr SW, 404-525-9212

www.thebusybeecafe.com

CUISINE: Soul Food

DRINKS: No Booze

SERVING: Lunch

PRICE RANGE: $$

NEIGHBOROOD: West End/Atlanta University

This old-school soul food eatery, around since 1947, is popular among locals and celebrities like Jay-Z. Here you'll find good home cooking serving favorites like collards, fried chicken and mac and cheese. Neck bones, anyone?

CAFÉ INTERMEZZO

1065 Peachtree Rd. NE, 404-355-0411

www.cafeintermezzo.com

CUISINE: Coffee & Tea, Desserts

DRINKS: Full Bar

SERVING: Lunch, Dinner

PRICE RANGE: $$

NEIGHBORHOOD: Midtown

They want you to think of this as a "European coffeehouse," but it's really just a big old tourist trap. "A visit is like stepping back over 100 years in Vienna." Well, no it's not. Gigantic 50-page menu has everything you can imagine and over 100 pastries. Impressive wine, Champagne and beer selection.

CAKES & ALE

155 Sycamore St., Decatur, 404-377-7994
www.cakesandalerestaurant.com
CUISINE: American (New); Italian
DRINKS: Full Bar
SERVING: Dinner
PRICE RANGE: $$$
NEIGHBORHOOD: Decatur

A restaurant and bakery, both equally impressive, offering unassuming food using the highest quality ingredients. Lasagna with lamb ragu, squid braised in red wine, trout cooked in a wood-burning oven and then served with a bacon & onion mayo. Yum. Chef Billy Allin knows his stuff. Don't ignore the vegetables here—they get special treatment in the kitchen and results are quite unusual. (I could say the same for the desserts: this is one of those places where you could eat sides of vegetables followed by a dessert and be completely satisfied. Take a look at the shamelessly rich layer cakes and tell me I'm wrong.)

CANTON HOUSE
4825 Buford Hwy NE, Chamblee, 770-936-9030
www.cantonhouserestaurant.com
CUISINE: Dim Sum
DRINKS: Beer & Wine
SERVING: Lunch & Dinner
PRICE RANGE: $$
NEIGHBORHOOD: Chamblee
Casual eatery featuring a menu of dim sum and traditional
Cantonese cuisine. Menu favorites include: Pork
dumplings; Chicken feet; shrimp wrapped in fried tofu
skin; rice noodle rolls stuffed with shrimp; radish cakes;
Chinese sausage wrapped in lotus leaf.

CHAI PANI
406 W. Ponce de Leon Ave, Atlanta, 404-378-4030
www.chaipanidecatur.com
CUISINE: Indian
DRINKS: Full Bar
SERVING: Lunch & Dinner
PRICE RANGE: $$
NEIGHBORHOOD: Decatur
Cute little café serving Indian "street food" and traditional
Indian cuisine. Menu favorites include: Samosa
smothered in tamarind and mint chutney. Vegan and
gluten-free options available.

CHOPS LOBSTER BAR
70 W. Paces Ferry Rd. NW, 404-262-2675
www.buckheadrestaurants.com/
CUISINE: American; steakhouse
DRINKS: Full Bar
SERVING: dinner

PRICE RANGE: $$$
NEIGHBORHOOD: Buckhead
Steak tartare, bone-in ribeye, double Porterhouse,
Kurobuta pork chop. Next to the St. Regis.

CHROME YELLOW TRADING CO.

501 Edgewood Ave SE, 470-355-1340
www.chromeyellowtradingco.com
CUISINE: Coffee & Tee
DRINKS: No Booze
SERVING: Breakfast, Lunch, Dinner
PRICE RANGE: $$
NEIGHBORHOOD: Old Fourth Ward
Unique mixture of a coffee shop up in the front and retail
shop offering trendy men's & women's fashions as well
as ceramics. Coffee shop offers variety of coffees, teas,
and pastries. Dog-friendly patio. The coffee beans come
from Stumptown.

COLONNADE

1879 Cheshire Bridge Rd. NE, 404-874-465
No web site
CUISINE: American, Southern
DRINKS: Full Bar
SERVING: lunch / dinner
PRICE RANGE: $$
NEIGHBORHOOD: Morningside/Lenox Park
A popular family restaurant that is always filled with
locals. Southern cooking at its finest, serving typical
favorites like fried chicken, collard greens and mac-n-
cheese. Giant portions. Excellent prime rib. Delicious
desserts like strawberry shortcake with ice cream.

EL RAY DEL TACO
Pinetree West Shopping Center, 5288 Buford Hwy NE,
Doraville, 770-986-0032
www.elreydeltacoatl.com
CUISINE: Mexican
DRINKS: Beer & Wine
SERVING: Lunch & Dinner (open late)
PRICE RANGE: $
NEIGHBORHOOD: Doraville
A favorite late-night haunt known for its excellent
Mexican platters and tacos. You can watch them in the
kitchen making the corn tortillas to order. Menu favorites
include: Lengua (tongue) and carnita tacos.

EATS
600 Ponce De Leon Ave. NE, 404-888-9149
www.eatsonponce.net
CUISINE: Southern, Italian, Caribbean
DRINKS: Beer & Wine
SERVING: Lunch, Dinner

PRICE RANGE: $
NEIGHBORHOOD: Old Fourth Ward
An Atlanta mainstay offering a menu of healthy foods and homestyle staples like jerk and BBQ chicken, fettucini Alfredo and fresh vegetarian dishes.

EMPIRE STATE SOUTH
999 Peachtree St. NE, 404-541-1105
www.empirestatesouth.com
CUISINE: Southern; New Southern
DRINKS: Full Bar
SERVING: Breakfast, Lunch, Dinner
PRICE RANGE: $$$
NEIGHBORHOOD: Midtown
A community restaurant serving authentic Southern dishes focusing on the foods of the region. Try the oyster

po'boy. But they have lots of other things you won't see on menus in Atlanta, like crispy sweetbreads and lamb belly with braised cabbage. When was the last time you had chicken consommé, at your granny's house? Here it's served with meatballs, boiled peanuts and root veggies. Yum. Chef here is Hugh Acheson, a judge on "Top Chef." Extensive coffee bar.

EUGENE
2277 Peachtree Rd. NE, 404-355-0321
www.restauranteugene.com
CUISINE: New American
DRINKS: Full Bar
SERVING: Dinner
PRICE RANGE: $$$$
NEIGHBORHOOD: Midtown

This place is properly styled "Restaurant Eugene," but I don't like the way it alphabetizes, so it's here under the E's. This place has a beautiful ambience and elegant décor but more important, the food is delicious and for the most part made from fresh ingredients. Southern cooking taken to the next level. Great service. Considered one of the best places in town. Take the fried chicken—here it's cooked in a witch's brew of savory animal fats. The resulting product will melt in your mouth.

FARM BURGER
3365 Piedmont Rd. NE, 404-816-0603
www.farmburger.net
CUISINE: Burgers
DRINKS: Beer & Wine
SERVING: Lunch, Dinner
PRICE RANGE: $$
NEIGHBORHOOD: Buckhead
As the name implies, here it's all about the burgers, which are made from 100% fresh grass-fed beef. The menu is seasonal and sourced from local farms. You must try the Spicy Garlic and Parmesan Fries.

FAT MATT'S RIB SHACK
1811 Piedmont Ave NE, 404-607-1622
www.fatmattsribshack.com
CUISINE: Barbeque
DRINKS: Beer & Wine
SERVING: Lunch, Dinner
PRICE RANGE: $$
NEIGHBOROOD: Morningside/Lenox Park
It's a hole-in-the-wall but worth a visit. The food is good, cheap and messy. Great ribs. Live Blues Music.

FELLINI'S PIZZA

4429 Roswell Rd. NE, 404-303-8248

www.fellinisatlanta.com

CUISINE: Pizza

DRINKS: Beer & Wine

SERVING: Lunch, Dinner

PRICE RANGE: $

NEIGHBORHOOD: several locations in Atlanta

Better than average pizza, ordered by the slice or pie.
Their white pizza is the best.

FLIP BURGER BOUTIQUE

3655 Roswell Rd. NE, 404-549-3298 - Buckhead

1587 Howell Mill Rd. NW, 404-343-1609 – West
Midtown

www.flipburgerboutique.com

CUISINE: Burgers, American (New), Wine Bars

DRINKS: Full Bar

SERVING: Lunch, Dinner

PRICE RANGE: $$

NEIGHBORHOOD: Buckhead – West Midtown

A modern burger boutique featuring a menu that redefines
what we've come to think a hamburger should be. In a
modern space, FLIP incorporates elements of fine dining
with a creative, raw energy. While they serve classic all-
American burgers, they also have some interesting twists:
try the Bun Mi, seared pork sausage with pickled ginger
and Asian-spiced cole slaw. Or try one of their liquid-
nitrogen milkshakes. You'll love the whimsicality of the
place: the designer has a pair of white banquettes upside
down to make a "roof" over the banquette you're sitting
in. Visually stunning and fun.

FRED'S MEAT & BREAD

99 Krog St NE, Atlanta, 404-688-3733

www.fredsmeatandbread.com/

CUISINE: Burgers/Sandwiches

DRINKS: No Booze

SERVING: Lunch & Dinner

PRICE RANGE: $$$

NEIGHBORHOOD: Old Fourth Ward

Small sandwich shop serves international specialties. What elevates the sandwiches here is that the chef uses only the best ingredients, so everything's top-notch. Menu favorites include: Pimiento Cheese Club and homemade fries. Simple, unpretentious comfort food.

THE GENERAL MUIR

Emory Point, 1540 Avenue Pl B-230, Atlanta, 678-927-9131

www.thegeneralmuir.com

CUISINE: American/Delis

DRINKS: Full Bar

SERVING: Breakfast, Lunch & Dinner

PRICE RANGE: $$

NEIGHBORHOOD: Emory Point

Upscale New York-style Jewish deli (with some pleasant twists on old classics) with a menu that won't disappoint. More fun for breakfast and lunch than later. Smoked salmon over latkes & sour cream; a skyscraper of a pastrami sandwich with lots of whole grain mustard; burgers with 2 patties, Russian dressing & American cheese; a delicious Rueben and Matzo Ball soup.

GRAND CHAMPION BBQ
99 Krog St NE, Atlanta, 404-467-4427
www.gcbbq.net/
CUISINE: Barbeque
DRINKS: Beer & Wine Only
SERVING: Lunch & Dinner
PRICE RANGE: $$
NEIGHBORHOOD: Roswell
BBQ counter-serve eatery with a menu featuring locally sourced meats. Menu favorites include: Baby back ribs and Redneck Lasagna. Known for their sauces.

GUNSHOW
924 Garrett St, Atlanta, 404-380-1886
www.gunshowatl.com
CUISINE: Southern; New American
DRINKS: Full Bar
SERVING: Dinner Tues – Sat from 6 to 9
PRICE RANGE: $$$
NEIGHBORHOOD: Glenwood Park
This is rock star Chef Kevin Gillespie's take on

a combination of Chinese dim sum and Brazilian churrascaria-style dining. I know of 2 or 3 places in the country where they have the guy who actually cooks the food bring it out to your table. In this way, you get to talk to the chef about the dish he's made. Here, they using rolling carts and trays and the chefs bring out what they've made for you to see. If you like it, you order it. It's a big open environment here, with communal style tables, a big open kitchen where you can see Kevin and his co-chefs working up a sweat. Menu changes daily, but it's always new and interesting. Well worth a stop. (When you see the red-bearded Chef Kevin roaming around the room, don't be embarrassed to ask for a photo with him. You won't be the first.) Kevin has a great cookbook, also: "Pure Pork Awesomeness."

HEIRLOOM MARKET BBQ
2243 Akers Mill Rd SE, 770-612-2502
www.heirloommarketbbq.com
CUISINE: Barbeque
DRINKS: No Booze
SERVING: Lunch, Dinner
PRICE RANGE: $$
NEIGHBOROOD: Smyrna/Vinings
Food is amazing here. Delicious mouth-watering ribs, pulled chicken and mac 'n cheese with red chili. The guys here make their ribs in the Korean style, rubbing the ribs with "gochujang" (a hot-n-spicy paste). They are quick to tell you that Korean BBQ was being

made 3,000 years before American was founded. (They have 5 varieties of sauces to try.) The catch is that because of a local ordinance this place is now take-out only, but you can eat standing up out on their patio in good weather.

HOLEMAN & FINCH
2277 Peachtree Rd. NE, 404-948-1175
www.holeman-finch.com

CUISINE: American (New), Gastropubs
DRINKS: Full Bar
SERVING: Dinner
PRICE RANGE: $$
NEIGHBORHOOD: Midtown

This is the cheaper eatery run by the chef of "**Restaurant Eugene**." Delicious food, great drinks, good vibe at a moderate price. The deviled eggs merit special attention: they're made with country ham, jalapeno and bread-and-butter pickles. I love offal, so I'm nuts over the veal brains and smoked sweetbreads. This place gets crowded so there's usually a wait for tables. The specialty double brisket & chuck cheeseburgers are a must served with house-made pickles. They used to make 24 a night, at 10 P.M. sharp—and they sold out in one minute flat. Now you can get them starting at 5 p.m. Definitely one of the coolest places in Atlanta.

HOMEGROWN

968 Memorial Dr. SE, 404-222-0455
www.homegrownga.com
CUISINE: Breakfast & Brunch, Vegetarian
DRINKS: No Alcohol
SERVING: Breakfast, Lunch
PRICE RANGE: $
NEIGHBORHOOD: East Atlanta

A "laid-back" coffee shop serving "top-notch" Southern food (breakfast all day) using fresh ingredients and locally grown produce.

JCT KITCHEN & BAR
1198 Howell Mill Rd., 404-355-2252
www.jctkitchen.com
CUISINE: Southern
DRINKS: Full Bar
SERVING: Lunch, Dinner, Brunch
PRICE RANGE: $$
NEIGHBORHOOD: West Midtown
Southern cooking at its best. Fried chicken, Shrimp &
Grits and North Georgia Trout are just a few of the tasty
menu selections. Live music Thurs. Fri. & Sat.

KEVIN RATHBUN STEAK HOUSE
154 Krog St. NE, 404-524-5600
www.kevinrathbunsteak.com
CUISINE: Steakhouse
DRINKS: Full Bar
SERVING: Dinner
PRICE RANGE: $$$$
NEIGHBORHOOD: Inman Park
In Inman Park, you'll find this top notch steakhouse with
an excellent wine list. This guy beat Bobby Flay on "Iron
Chef America." Here you'll see why: eggplant fries,
Coca-cola baby back ribs with a cabbage-scallion slaw
that's really tasty, a Maine lobster tail (half or whole)
served cold as a starter, dry aged cowboy ribeye (22 oz),
ribeye (10 or 20 oz), filets, strips, chops. Great sides, as
you'd expect: braised greens with hog jowl, twice-baked
potato, Parmesan fries. One of four of Kevin Rathbun's
Atlanta restaurants. All are worth visiting.

KIMBALL HOUSE
303 E Howard Ave, Decatur, 404-378-3502
www.kimball-house.com
CUISINE: New Southern

DRINKS: Full Bar
SERVING: Dinner
PRICE RANGE: $$$
NEIGHBORHOOD: Decatur

The bar here is really fun, as it's set in Decatur's old train station. High ceilings, tall windows that let in lots of light. The bar specializes in absinthe-based cocktails. An oyster lovers' haven, Kimball House offers as many varieties of the bivalve as the Oyster Bar in Grand Central Station. (Or so it seems.) Menu favorites include: Lobster & Artichoke tarte and Chicken Roulade, but since the menu changes daily, you're never sure. What you can be sure of, however, is the consistent high quality of the food here. Take the butter beans, a staple in many Southern diets. The French-trained chefs here glaze them with butter, lemon and garlic. The teeny bits of house-cured ham set this dish apart. You could eat a big bowl of them. If you have time for only one thing to do in Decatur, this would be my choice.

KING + DUKE

3060 Peachtree Rd, Atlanta, 404-477-3500
www.kinganddukeatl.com
CUISINE: American
DRINKS: Full Bar
SERVING: Lunch & Dinner
PRICE RANGE: $$$
NEIGHBORHOOD: Buckhead
Another restaurant from Chef Ford Fry, this eatery offers a seasonal dining experience. A 24-foot open hearth is the main focus of this restaurant as many of the dishes are cooked over wood. Menu favorites include: Yorkshire pudding, aged, bone-in rib eye and Mississippi rabbit with liver toast. Menu changes often.

LA FONDA LATINA

2813 Peachtree Rd. NE, 404-816-8311
www.fellinisatlanta.com
CUISINE: Cuban
DRINKS: Full Bar
SERVING: Lunch, Dinner
PRICE RANGE: $
NEIGHBORHOOD: several locations in Atlanta
Good solid Cuban food with dishes like the Cuban Sandwich platter that comes with black beans and rice. (I'm from Miami, so I know good Cuban food. This is v-e-r-y close.)

La Grotta Ristorante Italiano

LA GROTTA
2637 Peachtree Rd. NE, 404-231-1368
www.lagrottaatlanta.com
CUISINE: Italian
DRINKS: Full Bar
SERVING: Dinner
PRICE RANGE: $$$
NEIGHBORHOOD: Midtown
An Atlanta tradition since 1978, this eatery offers delicious fare in a beautiful atmosphere with great service. Voted Best Italian Restaurant for many years by *Atlanta Magazine*.

LADYBIRD GROVE & MESS HALL
684 John Wesley Dobbs Ave NE, Atlanta, 404-458-6838
http://www.ladybirdatlanta.com/
CUISINE: American (New)
DRINKS: Full Bar
SERVING: Lunch & Dinner
PRICE RANGE: $$
NEIGHBORHOOD: Old Fourth Ward

A hip rustic themed restaurant and bar with a menu of New American cuisine. Menu favorites include: Spatchcock Chicken and the Double decker burger. Don't leave without trying the Navajo Fry Bread. This dish starts out as a piece of bread that's fried until crispy. Then it's covered with Benton's country ham sliced thinly and topped with cilantro and some black pepper. Then, to provide contrast, honey is dribbled over the whole thing.

LEON'S FULL SERVICE
131 E Ponce De Leon Ave., Decatur, 404-687-0500
www.leonsfullservice.com
CUISINE: Gastropubs, American (Traditional)
DRINKS: Full Bar
SERVING: Lunch, Dinner
PRICE RANGE: $$
NEIGHBORHOOD: Decatur
The name says it all. At Full Service you get it all: great food and great service. Known for their specialty cocktails. Try the One-Eyed Jack: rye, root, maple and bitters. Superior beer list, including over a dozen on draft. (Try the local beer, Red Brick Porter.) worth going to Decatur. Menu selections include: chicken sausage, chickpea salad, veggie loaf and molasses toffee pudding.

LITTLE TART BAKESHOP
99 Krog St, 404-348-4797
www.littletartatl.com/
CUISINE: Coffee shop; pastries; light fare
DRINKS: Beer & wine
SERVING: Breakfast, Lunch, Dinner
PRICE RANGE: $$
NEIGHBORHOOD: Grant Park
Discovered this (as well as the **Octane** coffee shop) after visiting the Oakland Cemetery just a few feet away. Then I

remembered Anthony Bourdain mentioning the place in one of his shows. Ham and cheese croissant is the best. Among the sweet treats: their superior pecan pie and the strawberry galette.

MILLER UNION
999 Brady Ave., 678-733-8550
www.millerunion.com/
CUISINE: New Southern / American
DRINKS: Full bar
SERVING: Lunch, Dinner
PRICE RANGE: $$$
NEIGHBORHOOD: West Midtown
Chef Steven Satterfield (James Beard Award for Best Chef Southeast in 2017) bases his menu on ingredients available from week-to-week. Always a great experience if you're looking for the "new" in Southern cuisine. Cornmeal breaded fried oysters, braised pork cheeks, homemade pork and sage sausage, grilled Vidalia onions.

MINERO
Ponce City Market
675 Ponce De Leon Ave, N.E., Atlanta, 404-532-1580
www.minerorestaurant.com
CUISINE: Mexican
DRINKS: TBA
SERVING: TBA
PRICE RANGE: $$
NEIGHBORHOOD: Old Fourth Ward
Chef Sean Brock, famed for his Husk restaurants in Charleston and Nashville, is opening this Southern-Mexican spot. Expect things like tacos made with catfish and burritos with hoppin' John. Yes!

NO. 246

129 E Ponce De Leon Ave., Decatur, 678-399-8246
www.no246.com
CUISINE: Italian; New Southern
DRINKS: Full Bar
SERVING: Lunch, Dinner
PRICE RANGE: $$
NEIGHBORHOOD: Decatur
Here Chef Ford Fry (who also owns **JCT Kitchen and Bar**) has a restaurant that serves Italian-inspired cuisine composed of local, farm fresh ingredients. What he really does is fuse Italian with Southern cooking to create a new kind of cuisine you won't find anywhere else. Really. Try the broccoli soup with crispy pancetta and cheddar to start.

NORTHERN CHINA EATERY
5141 Buford Hwy NE, Atlanta, 770-458-2282
No Website
CUISINE: Chinese
DRINKS: No Booze
SERVING: Lunch & Dinner; closed Tues
PRICE RANGE: $
NEIGHBORHOOD: Doraville
Small put popular eatery. Lots of lamb dishes, and I especially like the cumin-rubbed skewers when they're the daily special. Menu favorites: Mandarin Pie (a pork dish) and Boiled cabbage with egg yolks; potato and carrot stir fry.

OCTANE COFFEE BAR

437 Memorial Dr, SE, 404-815-9886 – Grant Park
1009-B Marietta St – West Midtown
www.octanecoffee.com/
CUISINE: Coffee shop; pastries; light fare
DRINKS: Beer & wine
SERVING: Breakfast, Lunch, Dinner
PRICE RANGE: $$
NEIGHBORHOOD: Grant Park & West Midtown
Apple crisp tart is my favorite. Great place to slip into
after visiting the Oakland Cemetery across the street.

OLD BRICK PIT BARBEQUE

4805 Peachtree Rd, Chamblee, 770-986-7727
www.oldbrickpitbbq.com/
CUISINE: Barbeque
DRINKS: No Booze
SERVING: Lunch & Dinner; closed Sun
PRICE RANGE: $
NEIGHBORHOOD: Fairmont
Open since 1976, this place is known for their sauce
made from a family recipe. Simple menu featuring items
like pulled pork and ribs cooked in their hickory fired
pit, Brunswick stew and peach cobbler. The dressing on
the chopped pork has a spicy tomato tang to it you won't
soon forget. Make sure you get a side of the lovely sweet
cole slaw.

THE OPTIMIST
914 Howell Mill Rd., 404-477-6260
www.theoptimistrestaurant.com
CUISINE: Seafood; Southern
DRINKS: full bar
SERVING: Lunch, Dinner
PRICE RANGE: $$$
NEIGHBORHOOD: West Midtown
"Esquire" called this the best new restaurant in America
in 2012 ("Bon Appétit" did the same thing in 2013)
and it's easy to see why. The splendor is the room—a
cavernous white ceiling supported by exposed steel
trusses is most dramatic. There's an oyster bar with the
contours of a surfboard (serving over 20 varieties). My
feeling is that Chef Ford Fry owes a debt to some of
the more edgy culinary trends emanating from nearby
Charleston. This is why I recommend you try the she-crab
soup with shrimp toast, followed by the octopus cooked
Spanish style and served with watermelon before you dip

your fork ever so gently into the red snapper in a lovely lime broth. Or the redfish in a cornmeal crust. If you're not in a seafood mood, get the bone-in pork chop. If you worship seafood, this is your temple. This place will remind you of the fish camps your parents took you to by the lake when you were a kid.

PARISH
240 N. Highland Ave., 404-681-4434
www.parishatl.com
CUISINE: Southern, American
DRINKS: Full Bar
SERVING: Breakfast, Lunch, Dinner
PRICE RANGE: $$
NEIGHBORHOOD: Inman Park
The reputation as one of Atlanta's top restaurants is well deserved. Serving delicious fresh food with live music. Pan fried catfish, steak tartare, country ham and chicken liver paté. The buttermilk fried chicken comes with collard greens and corn bread.

PHO DAI LOL #2
4186 Buford Hwy NE Ste G, Atlanta, 404-633-2111
No Website
CUISINE: Vietnamese
DRINKS: No Booze
SERVING: Lunch & Dinner
PRICE RANGE: $
NEIGHBORHOOD: Druid Hills
Located in a little plaza, the food sets this Vietnamese eatery apart from the others. Menu features a variety of Pho dishes and noodles. You can customize your bowl with its rich beefy broth by adding cilantro, mint, chili sauce, eye-round steak, brisket. The possibilities are endless.

THE PIG & THE PEARL

1380 Atlantic Dr NW, Atlanta, 404-541-0930

www.thepigandthepearl.com/

CUISINE: Barbeque

DRINKS: Full Bar

SERVING: Lunch & Dinner

PRICE RANGE: $$

NEIGHBORHOOD: Atlantic Station

This family friendly eatery with a sleek modern look offers a simple menu of smokehouse fare along with oysters and crafted cocktails. Raw bar. The chef likes the word "smokehouse" over "BBQ" because he adds a bit of smoke to lots of different things, like chicken, beef brisket with hickory and pecan woods. As an appetizer, I'd recommend the lobster salad with tarragon. Patio seating available when temperatures allow.

POLARIS

265 Peachtree St NE, Atlanta, 404-460-6425

www.polarisatlanta.com

CUISINE: American

DRINKS: Full Bar

SERVING: Lunch & Dinner; closed Sun & Mon

PRICE RANGE: $$

NEIGHBORHOOD: Downtown

Located 22 stories atop the historic **Hyatt Regency Atlanta** hotel, this iconic rotating restaurant has been popular among tourists since the flying saucer-shaped revolving bar opened in 1967. It had gotten quite shabby and was closed in 2004 for a 10-year-long renovation job. Now even locals pop up for a drink and a look at the stunning view. I remember my first time up here. I didn't think there was anything to "see" in Atlanta. But I turned out to be wrong. Menu offers chef-inspired shared plates and handcrafted cocktails.

THE PORTER BEER BAR
1156 Euclid Ave. NE, 404-223-0393
www.theporterbeerbar.com
CUISINE: American (New), Pubs
DRINKS: Beer & Wine
SERVING: Lunch, Dinner & Brunch
PRICE RANGE: $$
NEIGHBORHOOD: Little Five Points
A new restaurant serving American cuisine with a menu of small plates and sandwiches. The beer bar features a menu of over 800 beers.

PURE TAQUERIA
300 N Highland Ave. NE, 404-522-7873
www.puretaqueria.com
CUISINE: Mexican, Sandwiches, Tex-Mex
DRINKS: Full Bar
SERVING: Lunch & Dinner
PRICE RANGE: $$
NEIGHBORHOOD: Inman Park
A new take on an authentic Mexican taqueria.
Sophisticated and fun with tasty margaritas. Five
locations in Atlanta.

QUOC HUONG BANH MI FAST FOOD
5150 Buford Hwy NE, Atlanta, 770-936-0605
No Website
CUISINE: Vietnamese
DRINKS: No Booze
SERVING: Lunch & Dinner; closed Thurs.
PRICE RANGE: $$$

NEIGHBORHOOD: Doraville

Popular eatery offering a menu of Vietnamese banh mi sandwiches and pho noodle soups. They are actually better known for their sandwiches with their extra crispy rice-flour baguettes. The most-ordered item here is the sandwich stuffed with crunchy BBQed pork that has a spicy kick. The sandwiches are even better when you add a fried egg. Delicious smoothies and bubble tea.

RATHBUN'S

112 Krog St. NE, 404-524-8280

www.rathbunsrestaurant.com/

CUISINE: New American

DRINKS: Full Bar

SERVING: Dinner

PRICE RANGE: $$$

NEIGHBORHOOD: Inman Park

This is Rathbun's flagship eatery with his upmarket take on some Southern classics in an industrial décor that's very slick. He has quite the mini-empire along Krog Street, and it's well deserved. Crispy duck breast, Thai risotto, flash-fried oysters (luscious), roasted bone marrow, elk chop, BBQ chicken with molasses and pepper—these are the standout dishes. Also here is **Krog Bar** (www.krogbar.com/), which has a great selection of small plates with lots of cheeses, charcuterie items, olives and little sandwiches on great bread.

RESTAURANT EUGENE
See "Eugene"
I only put this in here because one of my Atlanta writers, Colin Mathews, is such a stickler for details. Persnickety is probably a more accurate word. You know when you go to look up a hotel and the listing is under "Hotel Indigo" instead of "Indigo"? I'd look for "Indigo," not "Hotel Indigo." But not so our Sweet Colin. Thus, to placate his unified sensibility, here is the cross-reference.

RISING ROLL GOURMET
1180 W Peachtree St NW, Atlanta, 404-815-6787
www.risingroll.com
CUISINE: Deli/Sandwiches
DRINKS: No Booze
SERVING: Breakfast, Lunch
PRICE RANGE: $$
NEIGHBORHOOD: Downtown / Midtown, **several other locations**
This, perhaps the best deli in town, offers a menu of sandwiches, paninis, soups, salads and desserts. Portions are large and the specials are worth noting. Menu favorites include: Grilled chicken portabello panini and Mexicano chicken Panini.

SAGE WOODFIRE TAVERN
4505 Ashford Dunwoody, 770 804 8880
www.sagewoodfiretavern.com/
CUISINE: American

DRINKS: Full Bar
SERVING: Lunch weekdays; dinner from 5 (except Sunday, when it's closed)
PRICE RANGE: $$
NEIGHBORHOOD: North Perimeter Area
Fine dining, great elegant atmosphere. Shrimp bisque, a super meatloaf made with veal, beef and pork.

SERPAS
659 Auburn Ave. NE, 404-688-0040
www.serpasrestaurant.com
CUISINE: American (New); Creole, Southwestern, Asian fusion
DRINKS: Full Bar
SERVING: Lunch, Dinner, Brunch
PRICE RANGE: $$
NEIGHBORHOOD: Old Fourth Ward
Hip restaurant serving up New American fare with a Cajun inflection. Pigs in a blanket with homemade Andouille, flounder with gnocchi, duck confit. You'll love this massive dining room with its exposed pipes and hip industrial look.

SO BA VIETNAMESE
560 Gresham Ave SE, Atlanta, 404-627-9911
www.soba-eav.com
CUISINE: Vietnamese
DRINKS: Full Bar
SERVING: Dinner nightly, Lunch weekends
PRICE RANGE: $$$
NEIGHBORHOOD: East Atlanta Village
Typical Vietnamese eatery with a menu of classic Viet fare including pho, rice vermicelli and broken-rice dishes.

SOUTH CITY KITCHEN
1144 Crescent Ave. NE, 404-873-7358
www.southcitykitchen.com
CUISINE: Southern
DRINKS: Full Bar
SERVING: Lunch & Dinner
PRICE RANGE: $$$
NEIGHBORHOOD: Midtown
Serving fresh and contemporary new Southern cuisine for 19 years. One of Atlanta's favorite restaurants. Great dishes like: shrimp and grits, buttermilk fried chicken, she-crab soup, fried green tomatoes and banana pudding.

SOUTHERN ART & BOURBON BAR
Intercontinental
3315 Peachtree Rd. NE, 404-946-9070
www.southernart.com
CUISINE: American; New Southern
DRINKS: Full Bar
SERVING: Breakfast, Lunch, Dinner
PRICE RANGE: $$$
NEIGHBORHOOD: Buckhead
Located in the Intercontinental, Chef Art Smith offers
a menu of Southern comforts and traditional classics.
Try the Buttermilk fried chicken, which comes squash
casserole, garlic green beans and red pepper gravy.
There's also a "Ham Bar" offering a variety of pork
products. If there's room, check out the vintage dessert
table. Bar and lounge area.

SOUTHERN SOUL BARBEQUE

2020 Demere Rd, Saint Simons Island, 912-638-7685

www.southernsoulbbq.com/

CUISINE: Barbeque/Soul Food

DRINKS: Beer & Wine Only

SERVING: Lunch & Dinner

PRICE RANGE: $$

NEIGHBORHOOD: Saint Simons Island

Located in a former gas station, this Southern BBQ joint serves favorites like oak-smoked meat, BBQ turkey, pork shoulder and brisket.

SPICE TO TABLE

659 Auburn Ave NE #506, Atlanta, 404-220-8945

www.spicetotable.com/

CUISINE: Indian

DRINKS: No Booze

SERVING: Lunch & Dinner; closed Sun

PRICE RANGE: $$

NEIGHBORHOOD: Old Fourth Ward

Popular Indian eatery serving Indian patisserie and South Asian cuisine. Menu favorites include: Chicken and coconut rice wrapped in banana leaf and Mango Upside Down cake. They are famous for their version of the traditional carrot cake and fried chicken.

ST CECILIA
3455 Peachtree Rd, Atlanta, 404-554-9995
www.stceciliaatl.com
CUISINE: Seafood/Italian
DRINKS: Full Bar
SERVING: Lunch weekdays, Dinner nightly
PRICE RANGE: $$$
NEIGHBORHOOD: Buckhead
A friendly upscale eatery with a menu of Italian seafood and pasta offered in a glamorous venue with high ceilings soaring up 3 floors. Reclaimed woods in shades of color you never thought existed is used on the walls in a very dramatic space with white tiled columns. The 20-seat marble bar is my favorite place to hang out, of course. Not much of a Southern slant to the food, which leans more toward Asia and Europe for the menu's inspiration, which is fine with me. Menu favorites include: Rabbit pasta, smoky octopus with Italian bean salad & oregano, cobia crudo with trout roe. Impressive wine selection.

STAPLEHOUSE
541 Edgewood Ave SE, 404524-5005
www.staplehouse.com
CUISINE: American (New)
DRINKS: Full Bar
SERVING: Dinner, Brunch, closed Mon & Tues
PRICE RANGE: $$$
NEIGHBORHOOD: Old Fourth Ward
In this century-old brick building, you'll find the most unusual restaurant & and bar benefiting The Giving Kitchen charity offers a rotating seasonal menu. Herbs are grown on the patio. Chicken liver mousse is superior, beets served with house-cured bresaola are just perfect. Tables are reservations only with bar seats first come first served. Food is excellent if you're lucky enough to get a table. I always get there early and snatch a seat at the bar. (The Giving

Kitchen provides funds for people in the restaurant industry who have medical bills. All the profits after payroll and taxes go to the charity.)

SUNDIAL
Peachtree Center / Westin Hotel
210 Peachtree St. NW, 404 659-1400
www.sundialrestaurant.com/
CUISINE: American
DRINKS: Full Bar
SERVING: lunch / dinner
PRICE RANGE: $$
NEIGHBORHOOD: Downtown
The Sundial is the famous restaurant atop the Westin. It's certainly not famous for its food, but for the full view of Atlanta you get while you dine as the restaurant rotates 360 degrees.

SUSHI HOUSE HAYAKAWA

5979 Buford Hwy NE A10, Atlanta, 770-986-0010
www.atlantasushibar.com/
CUISINE: Japanese/Sushi
DRINKS: Full Bar
SERVING: Dinner; closed Mon & Tues
PRICE RANGE: $$$
NEIGHBORHOOD: Doraville
Classic Japanese eatery with a creative menu of sushi and
hot dishes. (One of the top 2 or 3 sushi places in Atlanta.)
Menu favorites include: Eel roll and Butabara (grilled
pork belly on a skewer).

SWALLOW AT THE HOLLOW

1072 Green St, Roswell, 678-352-1975
www.swallowatthehollow.com
CUISINE: Barbeque
DRINKS: Beer & Wine Only
SERVING: Lunch & Dinner; closed Mon & Tues
PRICE RANGE: $$
NEIGHBORHOOD: Roswell
Casual BBQ eatery offering a creative menu of dishes
like pulled pork and other pit-smoked items. A good place
to try regional sauces—the 3 here are N.C. vinegar, S.C.
mustard and Kansas City tomato. Menu favorites include:
Pit smoked portabella mushrooms and Fried Green
Tomatoes. Vegetarian options available.

TED'S MONTANA GRILL

133 Luckie St. NW, 404-521-9796

www.tedsmontanagrill.com

CUISINE: Burgers, American (Traditional)
DRINKS: Full Bar
SERVING: Lunch & Dinner
PRICE RANGE: $$
NEIGHBORHOOD: Downtown (plus 2 other locations in Midtown & Decatur)

Owned by Ted Turner (who often stops by for dinner), here you'll enjoy traditional American fare as well as treats like Buffalo burgers. All the burgers are top-notch. Friendly service.

TICONDEROGA CLUB

99 Krog St NE, 404-458-4534

www.ticonderogaclub.com

CUISINE: American (Traditional)/Cocktail bar
DRINKS: Full Bar
SERVING: Dinner, Brunch on Sunday, closed on Wed.
PRICE RANGE: $$
NEIGHBORHOOD: Inman Park

Cozy retro-inspired eatery in the Krog Street Market with a creative menu and tasty craft cocktails. Favorites: Dry aged roasted duck, Vietnamese shrimp skewers and Scallops with asparagus and celery root cream. Great selection of ciders and sherries. No reservations and it's often crowded.

TWO URBAN LICKS

820 Ralph McGill Blvd NE, 404-522-4622
www.twourbanlicks.com
CUISINE: American
DRINKS: Full Bar
SERVING: Dinner only
PRICE RANGE: $$$
NEIGHBORHOOD: Old Fourth Ward & Poncey-
Highlands area
Industrial chic décor. The "salmon chips" are a big
favorite here, but the fish tacos are good too. Pork spring
rolls, short ribs, Vidalia onion soup. Duck and lamb are
winners, too. Wine is on tap which is unique and there's
a huge selection. Amazing food, right off the Beltline
which afford a superior view.

THE VARSITY

61 North Ave NW, 404-881-1706
www.thevarsity.com
CUISINE: Fast Food
DRINKS: No Booze
SERVING: Lunch, Dinner
PRICE RANGE: $
NEIGHBOROOD: Midtown
This is the World's Largest Drive-in, with 800 seats,
stands on more than two acres. Nearly 30,000 people will
visit The Varsity during a Georgia Tech football game.
More than two miles of hot dogs, a ton of onion rings, and
5,000 homemade pies daily. The downtown location is the
world's largest single outlet for Coca-Cola. The dogs here
are served "naked," minus any toppings, or the best way:
with chili, cheese & cole slaw, which is something of a
tradition down South.

W. H. STILES FISH CAMP

Central Food Hall - Ponce City Market
675 Ponce de Leon Ave, Atlanta, 678-235-3929
http://www.starprovisions.com/whstilesfish-camp
CUISINE: Seafood
DRINKS: Beer & wine
SERVING: Brunch, Dinner
PRICE RANGE: $$$
NEIGHBORHOOD: Fairmont
A casual fish shack that is basically a sandwich shop but also serves creative salads and seafood. Menu favorites include: Shrimp boil, Steamed fish bowls, raw bar.

YALLA!

99 Krog St NE, 404-506-9999
www.yallaatl.com
CUISINE: Middle Eastern/Greek
DRINKS: No Booze
SERVING: Lunch, Dinner
PRICE RANGE: $$
NEIGHBORHOOD: Inman Park
Cute Middle Eastern food stall located next to Fred's Meat & Bread. A sandwich will feed 2 and often 3 people. Offerings: pita, laffa, and alla. Favorites: Spit roasted chicken and Israeli salad. Also excellent is the roasted lamb sandwich served with pickled turnips and rutabaga. Melts in your mouth.

Chapter 5
NIGHTLIFE

ALLEY CAT
50 Upper Alabama St. NW (*inside Underground Atlanta*),
678-904-2514
no web site at press time
NEIGHBORHOOD: Downtown
A nice dive bar place in Underground Atlanta with a rock
n' roll atmosphere, sexy waitresses.

DAD'S GARAGE
569 Ezzard St., SE Atlanta, 404 523 3141
www.dadsgarage.com
NEIGHBORHOOD: Little Five Points
Known as one of Atlanta's best venues for improv
comedy, original plays and other events. The audience can
even choose themes the comics have to work with.

CLERMONT LOUNGE
789 Ponce De Leon Ave. NE, 404-874-4783
www.clermontlounge.net / web site down at press time
NEIGHBORHOOD: Downtown East
The Clermont is Atlanta's oldest strip club and
consistently ranked as one of the coolest dive bars
anywhere. It's been around since 1965 and they pride
themselves on the fact you can bring your grandmother
here. Maybe that's because some of the dancers are
almost as old as grandma. One of the standout performers,
Blondie, is famous for demolishing beer cans with her…
well, you get the idea. Lots of fun. Cheap drinks, karaoke,
and live music.

COMPOUND
1008 Brady Ave. NW, 404-898-1702
www.compoundatl.com
NEIGHBORHOOD: West Midtown
A dance club with great music (usually hip-hop).

COSMOLAVA
45 13th St. NE, 404-873-6189
www.cosmolava.com
NEIGHBORHOOD: Midtown
A mega-bar with 3 levels, 6 bars, VIP accommodations
and some of the hottest DJs in the city. Four dance floors.
World-class DJs spin the latest House, Top 40, '80s, Funk
& Hip-Hop.

CYPRESS STREET PINT & PLATE
817 West Peachtree St. NE, 404-815-9243
www.cypressbar.com
NEIGHBORHOOD: Midtown
A restaurant and bar with a neighborhood pub vibe. Great
burgers and excellent selection of beers.

THE EARL
488 Flat Shoals Ave. SE, 404-522-3950
www.badearl.com
NEIGHBORHOOD: East Atlanta
This restaurant and lounge is known for its alternative
music. Good music and good food.

GOLD ROOM
2416 Piedmont Rd. NE, 404 400-5062
www.goldroomnightclub.com
NEIGHBORHOOD: Lindbergh
Upscale multi-level lounge and dance club in Lindbergh
Center that attracts a lively crowd.

HAVANA CLUB
3112 Piedmont Rd., 404-941-4847
www.havanaclubatl.com/

Web site down at press time
NEIGHBORHOOD: Buckhead
This big dance club has different rooms offering different
styles of music. But it's all fun.

LATITUDES BISTRO AND LOUNGE
100 CNN Center (*inside the Omni Hilton*), 404-659-0000
http://www.omnihotels.com/hotels/atlanta-cnn-center/dining/latitudes
NEIGHBORHOOD: Downtown
Great place to meet someone if you're one of the millions
of people attending a conference or convention, going to
a game or whatever. During the day, people drop in for
coffee, pastry, a light snack.

MJQ CONCOURSE
736 Ponce De Leon Ave. NE, 404-870-0575
No web site, but on Twitter & Facebook
NEIGHBORHOOD: Virginia Highlands
A club with an "underground" atmosphere that attracts a
young crowd. A two-room space located in an old parking
garage with a main basement room with a dance floor and
a lounge room. Music mostly old school hip-hop or '80s
& '90s with occasional bookings of blues and jazz acts.

MONDAY NIGHT BREWING
670 Trabert Ave NW, Atlanta, 404-352-7703
www.mondaynightbrewing.com
NEIGHBORHOOD: Westside / Home Park
An Atlanta-based craft brewery that brews balanced,
flavorful ales. It was opened by 3 guys who left the
corporate world to launch this place in the industrial-chic
Westside District. These guys used to meet every Monday
night to home-brew some beer, and now this.

NORTHSIDE TAVERN
1058 Howell Mill Rd. NW, 404-874-8745
www.northsidetavern.com
NEIGHBORHOOD: West Midtown
Voted one of the Top Ten Dive Bars in America. Great watering hole with cheap drinks and great music. Hosts some of the best local and regional Blues & Jazz acts.

OCTOPUS BAR
560 Gresham Ave SE, Atlanta, 404-627-9911
www.octopusbaratl.com/
NEIGHBORHOOD: East Atlanta
A late-night favorite of hipsters is this pub with an unmarked door nestled behind a "pho" house in East Atlanta. This graffiti-covered bar offers an impressive menu of wine and champagne. Nice simple menu of snacks like salt & pepper shrimp and Korean pork. Closed Sunday.

OPERA
1150 Crescent Ave. NE, 404-874-3006
www.operaatlanta.com/
NEIGHBORHOOD: Midtown
A club carved out of the old opera house. A big room that has to be seen. Large dance floors, second-floor opera boxes and a state-of-the-art DJ booth. Dress code applies.

THE PORTER BEER BAR
1156 Euclid Ave NE, 404-223-0393
www.theporterbeerbar.com
NEIGHBORHOOD: Little Five Points
Extensive menu of over 800 beers with excellent food as well. Offers a variety of special events from beer tastings and festivals, to classes and themed dinners.

PUNCHLINE COMEDY CLUB

280 Hilderbrand Dr., 404-252-5233

www.punchline.com

NEIGHBORHOOD: Sandy Springs

Been here since 1982. Over 3,000 comics have performed in this, the granddaddy of Atlanta comedy venues.

SOUND TABLE

483 Edgewood Ave, SE, 404-835-2534

www.thesoundtable.com

NEIGHBORHOOD: Downtown

A funky two-level dining spot that transforms into a late-night club. Kitchen open until midnight. Dancing and great music.

SUTRA LOUNGE

1136 Crescent Ave. NE, 404-607-1160

sutraloungeatl.com/

NEIGHBORHOOD: Midtown

Top 40, hip hop bar. Great place to meet, flirt and maybe get lucky.

THE TABERNACLE

152 Luckie St. NW, 404-659-9022

www.tabernacleatl.com

NEIGHBORHOOD: Downtown

This mid-sized concert hall has hosted notable acts like Guns N' Roses, The Black Crowes, Fergie and Adele, Lenny Kravitz, Counting Crows. In 1910,this building was a tabernacle. Intimate venue insures you get close to the artists.

TONGUE AND GROOVE

2420 Piedmont Rd, 404-261-2325

www.tandgonline.com/

NEIGHBORHOOD: Buckhead

This popular dance club in the Lindbergh Center off Piedmont Road in Buckhead offers hip hop, R&B, good range of music in a very elegant, sleek setting. Good bartenders, right on top of things. Has 8,500 square feet of things going on. Very sharp place.

TWO URBAN LICKS

820 Ralph McGill Blvd. NE, 404-522-4622

www.twourbanlicks.com

NEIGHBORHOOD:

Known as the "club with food." A great night out with live music that includes great food. Free valet parking.

Chapter 6
GAY NIGHTLIFE

Midtown is arguably the heart of gay life in Atlanta, particularly centered around the corner of **10th** and **Piedmont/Juniper**.

BLAKE'S ON THE PARK
227 10th St. NE, 404-892-5786
www.blakesontheparkatlanta.com/
NEIGHBORHOOD: Midtown
Lots of great music here in this bustling place. They have 24 video monitors. Also has a pretty good wide-ranging menu with everything from good burgers, wraps, salads,

Chicago style hot dog, sandwiches (French dip and grilled cheese) and egg dishes (my favorite is the Hangover sandwich: 2 fried eggs, sausage & American cheese on a toasted roll).

BULLDOG BAR

893 Peachtree St. NE, 404-872-3025
No web site at press time.
NEIGHBORHOOD: Midtown
Big black club here in Atlanta. Small dance floor, so if you can't bump up against someone, you're not really trying.

BURKHART'S PUB

1492 Piedmont Ave. NE, 404-872-4403
www.burkharts.com
NEIGHBORHOOD:
This place, beside being a jam-packed gay bar (with karaoke, pool tables, event nights), also offers food. Lots of fried appetizers of the pub fare sort, but further down the menu you'll find thick burgers and salads and a very good rib eye for $16 (comes with veggie of the day and choice of potato).

THE EAGLE
306 Ponce de Leon Ave., 404-873-2453
www.atlantaeagle.com
NEIGHBORHOOD: Midtown/Old Fourth Ward
A dark leather bar where fetishes are welcome. An Atlanta institution. Dance floor. Outdoor deck. Friendly crowd.

THE HERETIC
2069 Cheshire Bridge Rd. NE, 404-325-3061
www.hereticatlanta.com
NEIGHBORHOOD:
A gay dance bar with an edge. Here you'll find TV screens showing nude male models and a leather shop in he back. Wednesday night is fetish night so you have to dress the part.

JUNGLE
2115 Faulkner Rd NE, 404-844-8800
http://www.jungleatl.com/
NEIGHBORHOOD: Buckhead
A warehouse-sized gay dance club that offers a variety of theme nights, great Wednesday night drag shows, and guest DJs. Great music and great dance floor.

MARY'S

1287 Glenwood Ave., 404-624-4411

www.marysatlanta.com

NEIGHBORHOOD: East Atlanta

Consistently voted one of the best gay bars (and dance clubs) not only in Atlanta, but the whole country. Karaoke (over 15,000 songs), DJs, everything; it's all here. Full schedule.

MY SISTER'S ROOM

1271 Glenwood Ave., 678-705-4585
www.mysistersroom.com
NEIGHBORHOOD: Grant Park
Best lesbian bar in Atlanta. Dance floor, good music. $5 cover.

OSCAR'S

1510 Piedmont Ave. NE, 404-815-8841
www.oscarsatlanta.com/
NEIGHBORHOOD: Midtown at Ansley Square
This is a big gay "martini & video bar." Full weekly schedule. Check web site for details.

SWINGING RICHARDS

1400 Northside Dr NW, 404-352-0532
www.swingingrichards.com
NEIGHBORHOOD: Westside/Home Park
This Atlanta institution serves up some of the hottest male studs you've ever seen and they are all wonderfully nude. No cover on Tuesday before midnight. Sorry ladies but it's men only.

WOOFS

2425 Piedmont Rd NE, 404-869-9422
www.woofsatlanta.com
NEIGHBORHOOD: Midtown
Woofs is a gay sports bar. Lots of flatscreen TVs for sports fans. Game nights. Decent bar food and friendly crowd.

Chapter 7
WHAT TO SEE & DO

ATLANTA CITYPASS

www.citypass.com

Get one of these to save time and money on some of the
bigger attractions in town. Adults $74, kids $54.
The Georgia Aquarium
World of Coca-Cola
Inside CNN Atlanta Studio Tour

Zoo Atlanta or Atlanta History Center
Fernbank Museum of Natural History or High Museum of
Art

APEX (AFRICAN-AMERICAN PANORAMIC EXPERINCE) MUSEUM

135 Auburn Ave, Atlanta, 404-523-2739
www.apexmuseum.org
NEIGHBORHOOD: Downtown
HOURS: Tues–Sat, 10 a.m. – 5 p.m.
ADMISSION: Moderate fee

APEX is a museum focusing on Auburn's history
through exhibits, replicas & workshops. Museum features
exhibitions, self-guided tours, and special presentations.
There's an exhibit with life-sized reproductions that
show you the condition slaves endured, including one
that replicates how they were packed into slave ships
for transport to the New World. There's an exhibit that
emphasize the creations of black inventors. They range
from the engineer that invented the traffic light to how
Michael Jackson created some of the special effects used
in his shows. Permanent and traveling exhibitions. The
Trolley Theater features a replica of the old trolley of
Auburn Avenue and a multimedia history presentation.

THE ATLANTA CYCLORAMA & CIVIL WAR MUSEUM

Grant Park, 800 Cherokee Ave SE, Atlanta, 404-658-7625
www.atlantacyclorama.org/
HOURS: Tues – Sat, 9:15 a.m.-4:30 p.m.
ADMISSION: Modest fee
The cyclorama takes you on a journey through time.
Experience the Battle of Atlanta during the American
Civil War.

CENTER FOR PUPPETRY ARTS
1404 Spring St NW, Atlanta, 404-873-3391
www.centerforpuppetryarts.com
NEIGHBORHOOD: Midtown
HOURS: Open daily
ADMISSION: Tickets sold for performances
A unique cultural experience for both children and adults.
Enjoy the wonder and art of puppetry. The center offers
performances, workshops and a hands-on museum

CNN CENTER
www.cnn.com/tour/
190 Marietta St., NW Atlanta, 404-827-2300
NEIGHBORHOOD: Downtown
It's easy to buy tickets online. Or see **Atlanta
CityPass**. The atrium at the entrance of the CNN Center
offers a few gift shops on the lower level. A great spot for
buying souvenirs that display Georgia and TBS network
logo merchandise, including CNN, HLN and Cartoon
Network characters at the CNN Store.

EBENEZER BAPTIST CHURCH
407 Auburn Ave. NW, 404-688-7300
www.historicebenezer.org
NEIGHBORHOOD: Downtown
A designated national historic site. This is the original church where
Marin Luther King, Jr., and his father preached. The Gothic Revival
building reopened in 2011 after a major restoration effort that made
it look like it did in the 1960s when the Kings worked here. (The
microphones in the pulpit are the originals used back then.)

FOX THEATER
660 Peachtree St NE, Atlanta, 404-881-2100
www.foxtheatre.org

The historic Fox Theatre is a mammoth 4,678 seat theater that offers more than 300 performances a year including everything from Broadway to rock n roll performances. The 1929 theatre was originally built as a movie house, but it's worth a show on its own, and you can book a guided tour of the elaborate facility famous for its Egyptian design themes run amok.

GEORGIA AQUARIUM
225 Baker St. NW, 404-581-4000
www.georgiaaquarium.org
NEIGHBORHOOD: Downtown

Modest admission fee; buy tickets online so you don't wait in line.
TIP: do yourself a favor and go early, as it gets crowded. To really enjoy, plan on 3 hours.

Within its 10 million gallons of water, this Aquarium—an aquatic zoo, really—houses 120,000 animals representing 500 species, including 4 young whale sharks, beluga whales (the white cute ones), bottlenose dolphins and manta rays. **Dolphin Tales** is a show that features dazzling special effects (and, oh, yes, dolphins). Don't overlook the **Journey with Gentle Giants** program that lets you scuba (or snorkel if you're not certified to dive) with whale sharks. This was the world's largest aquarium when it opened in 2005.

HIGH MUSEUM OF ART

1280 Peachtree St. NE, 404-733-4444

www.high.org

NEIGHBORHOOD: Midtown

The leading art museum in the Southeastern United States. After its $130 million, three-building expansion, the High Museum has gained world-class status. Notable is its renowned collection of classic and contemporary art and award-winning architecture by Renzo Piano. Collections consist of more than 12,000 pieces and include 19th and 20th century American and decorative art, significant European pieces, modern and contemporary art, photography, African art and Southern folk art (on top floor). Entrance fee.

HISTORIC FOURTH WARD PARK

680 Dallas St NE, Atlanta, 404-546-6757

www.h4wpc.com/

Atlanta's Historic Fourth Ward Park is a popular spot and features a large stormwater retention pond where there are ducks the kids can feed. A large playground also for kids. The park extends from Ponce City Market south to Freedom Parkway and the Carter Center.

JIMMY CARTER PRESIDENTIAL LIBRARY AND MUSEUM

441 Freedom Parkway, Atlanta, 404-865-7100
www.jimmycarterlibrary.gov/J
HOURS: Open Daily
ADMISSION: Moderate fee, Senior, military, students, and children are free

The library and museum holds U.S. President Jimmy Carter's papers and material relating to the Carter administration. The library is actually a research facility and museum holding approximately 27 million pages of Jimmy Carter's White House material including correspondence, memoranda, photographs, film, and videotape.

KENNESAW MOUNTAIN NATIONAL BATTLEFIELD PARK

900 Kennesaw Mountain Dr, Kennesaw, 770-427-4686
www.nps.gov/kemo/
Hours: Open daily

This park contains a Civil War battleground of the Atlanta Campaign and Kennesaw Mountain.

KROG STREET MARKET
99 Krog St, Atlanta, 770-434-2400
www.krogstreetmarket.com
NEIGHBORHOOD: Inman Park
A could of blocks east of the famous **Sweet Auburn Curb Market** is this popular 9-acre mixed-use space is filled with market stalls that sell produce, goods, prepared food, Southern-grown restaurants and a few retailers. I like **Grand Champion Barbecue**, where you can get both pulled pork and brisket versions, as well as **Xocolatl Small Batch Chocolate** and **Craft**, a Japanese eatery specializing izakaya, a Japanese place that serves food while the real emphasis is on the drinks.

MARTIN LUTHER KING JR. NATIONAL HISTORIC SITE
450 Auburn Ave. NE, 404-331-5190
www.nps.gov/malu/index.htm
NEIGHBORHOOD: Downtown
A National Historic Site consisting of several buildings surrounding Martin Luther King, Jr.'s boyhood home on Auburn Avenue in the Sweet Auburn historic district, which for many years has been the epicenter of African-American businesses. The original Ebenezer Baptist Church is also part of the national historic site that covers some 42 acres, as well as Fire Station No. 6, and a gift shop. King and wife Coretta are buried in the **King Center**, where you can buy tickets to his birthplace. The Victorian house contains telling details that bring him to life. Did you know he was a champion player of the game Monopoly?

MUSEUM OF DESIGN

1315 Peachtree St. NE, 404-979-6455

www.museumofdesign.org

NEIGHBORHOOD: Midtown

Known as MODA, this is the only museum in the Southeast devoted exclusively to the study and celebration of all things design. Featured exhibitions include architecture, industrial and product design, interiors and furniture, graphics, and fashion. Moderate admission fee.

NATIONAL CENTER FOR CIVIL AND HUMAN RIGHTS

100 Ivan Allen Jr. Blvd, Atlanta, 678-999-8990

www.civilandhumanrights.org

HOURS: Open daily

ADMISSION: Moderate admission fee

This cultural attraction is referred to as a "must-see" and "truly inspiring." A powerful and interactive museum that connects the American Civil Rights Movement to today's Global Human Rights Movements. One particularly moving exhibit demonstrates what black students endured during the "lunch counter" protests of the '60s, when they demanded to be served alongside white people. You wear a set of headphones, and when you place your hands on the counter, you hear the threats of the taunting whites that get louder and more angry and aggressive the longer you sit there. There are other exhibits emphasizing the struggles of other minorities like gays, women in Iran, the disabled, immigrants, etc.

OAKLAND CEMETERY
248 Oakland Ave. SE, 404-688-2107
www.oaklandcemetery.com
NEIGHBORHOOD: Downtown Southeast
During the 19th Century, the "rural garden" cemetery
movement emerged as an alternative to crowded
graveyards. Oakland exemplifies this movement. Here
you'll find the tombs of 70,000 people, including the
city's earliest inhabitants, as well as rich families with big
tombstone markers. You can buy a map for $4 that shows
you who's where, including the unprepossessing gravesite
of "Gone With the Wind" novelist Margaret Mitchell.
Also note the nearly 4,000 gravesites marked "CSA,"
which stands for Confederate States Army.

PIEDMONT PARK

1342 Worchester Dr NE, Atlanta, 404-875-7275

www.piedmontpark.org

NEIGHBORHOOD: Virginia Highland

A 189-acre urban park that features miles of paved paths available for walking, running, biking and inline skating. Popular destination for weekend picnics. Picnic shelters, tables, benches and grills available throughout the park. Play area for children located near 12th Street Gate. Recreational areas available include: 12 lighted tennis courts, two softball fields, two soccer fields, two beach volleyball courts and swimming center. The park also has a lake where you can fish. The park hosts a variety of annual celebrations and events including: Atlanta Pride Festival, Screen on the Green film series, the Atlanta Jazz Festival, the Atlanta Dogwood Festival, Georgia Shakespeare Festival, Music Midtown, and Festival Peachtree Latino.

STONE MOUNTAIN

1000 Robert E. Lee Blvd., Stone Mountain; 800-401-2407

www.stonemountainpark.com

NEIGHBORHOOD: Half-hour east of Atlanta

A quartz monzonite dome monadrock known for the enormous bas-relief on its north face, the largest bas-relief in the world. The carving depicts three figures of the Confederate States of America: Stonewall Jackson, Robert E. Lee and Jefferson Davis. The summit of the mountain can be reached by a walk-up trail on the west side or by the Skyride aerial tram. They also have a ropes course out here for serious climbers.

WOODRUFF ARTS CENTER

1280 Peachtree St NE, Atlanta, 404-733-4200

https://www.woodruffcenter.org

NEIGHBORHOOD: Downtown

ADMISSION varies per event

This is one of the largest arts center in the world and home to the Tony Award-winning Alliance Theatre, the Grammy Award-winning Atlanta Symphony Orchestra and the High Museum of Art, the leading art museum in the Southeast. This is a major visual and performing arts center. (The Woodruff in the name is for Robert Woodruff, who made his fortune in Coca-Cola.)

WORLD OF COCA-COLA MUSEUM
121 Baker St. NW, 404-676-5151
www.worldofcoca-cola.com
NEIGHBORHOOD: Downtown
Here you'll learn everything about Coke you ever wanted
to know (and probably a whole lot more). Permanent
exhibition tells the history of the Coca-Cola Company.
They'll even show you the vault where they keep the
secret recipe. Here you can try more than 60 products
made by the company. (These are from all over the world,
and you'll be surprised how much there is to see in this
place. Try Manzana Lift sold in Chile or the drink Beverly
marketed in Italy that has a bitter, bitter, bitter taste.)
Moderate admission fee.

Chapter 8
SHOPPING & SERVICES

AMERICASMART
240 Peachtree St, NW, 800-ATL-MART
www.americasmart.com/
NEIGHBORHOOD:
AmericasMart is comprised of four buildings that are
open **to trade only**: the Atlanta Gift Mart, Atlanta
Merchandise Mart, Atlanta Apparel Mart and Inforum.
Each year, AmericasMart hosts more than 400,000

retailers from every state and more than 70 countries around the world in 17 home furnishings, gift, floor covering and apparel markets.

ATLANTA MADE
1187 Howell Mill Rd NW, Atlanta, 855-285-6233
www.atlantamade.us
NEIGHBORHOOD: East Atlanta
A unique showroom that only sells products designed and made in the Atlanta metro area, representing some 70 local craftsmen and their paintings, photographs, furniture, jewelry, sculptures, interesting ceramic pieces, and skin care products and even dog treats.

ATLANTA VISION OPTICAL
1215 Caroline St., Suite H 100, 404-522-8886
AtlVisionOptical.com
NEIGHBORHOOD: Near Inman Park and Candler Park.
Exclusive high-end eyewear is available from very unique
lines from around the world. VIP room available for
exclusive clients with very high-end eyewear. The owner
has her own eyewear line that consists of unique materials
such as leather, gold, white gold and water buffalo horn.

BILLY REID
1170 Howell Mill Rd. NW, 877-757-3934
www.billyreid.com
NEIGHBORHOOD: Westside
Westside Provisions District, connected to the similarly
red-bricked **Westside Urban Market** by a bridge you walk
across.
This area used to be known for abandoned mills, stockyards
and warehouses until recent renovations brought in some
of the best shopping in town. Designer Billy Reid's
2,500 square-foot place offers both men's and women's
collections. The store also includes signature antique
aesthetic, complete with vintage photographs, salvaged
wood, old-fashioned furniture, flea-market finds and
Southern-themed wall coverings. (The Westside Provisions
District is a group of shops and boutiques housed in what
used to be a meatpacking facility.)

CACAO CAFÉ
1046 N Highland Ave NE, 404-892-8202 – Virginia-
Highlands
CACAO
202 Permalume Place, 404-221-9090

www.cacaoatlanta.com

2 locations

Handcrafted chocolates at their best. This is a "bean-to-bar" chocolate maker, producing every chocolate product from the cocoa bean. Chocolate-dipped fruit, handmade truffles. (The "Italian Cowboy" is made with espresso and bourbon.) Great gifts.

CNN CENTER

www.cnn.com/tour/

190 Marietta St NW, 404-827-2300

NEIGHBORHOOD: Downtown

It's easy to buy tickets online. Or see **Atlanta CityPass**. The atrium at the entrance of the CNN Center offers a few gift shops on the lower level. A great spot for buying souvenirs that display Georgia and TBS network logo merchandise, including CNN, HLN and Cartoon Network characters at the CNN Store.

FARMERS MARKETS

In **Buckhead** you'll find the **Peachtree Road Farmers Market**

2744 Peachtree Rd NW, 404-365-1078

www.peachtreeroadfarmersmarket.com

It has great produce, made-to-order crepes, wood-fired pizzas. The booths are arranged in a large oval shape so you can walk through the inside ring and then the outside. In the **Poncey-Highland** area, try out the **Freedom Farmers' Market at the Carter Center** – www.freedomfarmersmkt.com - a smaller market, but lots of fun. In the **Morningside**

– Lenox Park area, go to the **Morningside Farmers' Market** – www.morningsidemarket.com - this is the only market that's open year-round. It was the first to go all-organic. Only has about 15 vendors, but it's plenty.

JONATHAN ADLER
1198 Howell Mill Rd NW, 404-367-0414
www.jonathanadler.com
NEIGHBORHOOD: Midtown West
Shop dedicated to the iconic potter, designer, author, and personality Jonathan Adler. This home furnishings shop is filled with all things

Jonathan Adler including his famous ceramic collections, pillows featuring psychedelic prints that will take you back to the '60s, gorgeous glass lamps, unusual vases.

LENOX SQUARE MALL
3393 Peachtree Rd. NE, 404-233-6767
www.simon.com/mall/lenox-square
NEIGHBORHOOD: buckhead

Across from **Phipps Plaza** and anchored by Neiman Marcus, Bloomingdale's and Macy's, this mall is a popular mall for chain-store shopping in Atlanta. Stores include upscale Hermes, Burberry, Louis Vuitton, Cartier and David Yurman, mid-high range stores like Kate Spade, Coach and Polo, mid-range stores like Banana Republic, Kenneth Cole, J. Crew, Abercrombie, Aldo and Urban

Outfitters, and a few mid-low range stores such as the Gap. Also has a large Apple store. Outside of and next to the mall is a strip of stores which includes a number of boutiques including Blue Gene's.

ONWARD RESERVE
3072 Early St NW - Ste 100, Atlanta, 888-543-5022
http://onwardreserve.com/
NEIGHBORGHOOD: Buckhead
Excellent store for upwardly mobile Atlanta yuppies. It has the feel of a modern hunting lodge, with the deer antler mounted on the wall—look for Southern preppy clothing from dozens of designers: Cotton Snaps, Castaway, Brackish, duck Head, Barbour, Dubarry, Peter Millar, southern Proper. Outerwear, shirts, pants, jewelry—a vast array of clothing for men.

PARIS ON PONCE
716 Ponce De Leon Pl NE, Atlanta, 404-249-9965
www.parisonponce.com
NEIGHBORGHOOD: Old Fourth Ward / Virginia Highland
For many years, this has been a favorite bohemian destination. This 46,000 square foot venue (divided up into 3 buildings) showcases art, antiques, furnishings, ateliers, boutiques, and oddities. You'll find everything from vintage Americana to French candelabra. From bargains to expensive investment pieces, a variety of venders selling treasures of all levels of quality and price point. (The **Pop Marché** market section has over 30 indie boutiques.) The event-performance space here, **Le Maison Rouge**, is decorated to look like a cabaret from the Belle Epoque—well worth a look. You'll spend a day here just looking and another day shopping.

PHIPPS PLAZA MALL
3500 Peachtree Rd NE, 404-261-7910
www.simon.com/
NEIGHBORHOOD: Buckhead
Anchored by Saks Fifth Avenue, Nordstrom and Belk, this upscale mall has higher-end chain stores such as Barney's Co-op, Intermix, Versace, Armani, Gucci, Jimmy Choo and Tiffany's, including the only Jeffrey store outside of New York, as well as an AMC movie theater.

PONCE CITY MARKET
675 Ponce de Leon Ave, Atlanta, 404-900-7900
www.poncecitymarket.com
NEIGHBORHOOD: Buckhead
Ponce City Market breathes new life into the historic Sears, Roebuck & Co. building in Atlanta. The classic structure, which is the area's largest adaptive reuse project, has been reinvented as a vibrant community hub that houses Central Food Hall, various shops, flats and offices, all while pointing back to the roots of its inception. Only a few stores were open at press time, including **Onward Reserve**, **Anthropologie** and **West Elm**, but there's a LOT more to come, believe me.

THE SHOPS - BUCKHEAD ATLANTA
3035 Peachtree Rd, Atlanta, 678-704-0900
www.buckhead-atl.com
An outdoor shopping area boasting a unique collection of shops and restaurants. The 8-acre complex took about a decade to complete. Some of the shops include **Shake Shack** (Georgia's first location), **Hermes, Brunello Cucinelli, Christian Louboutin, Le Bilboquet, American Food and Beverage, Thirteen Pies** and **Warby Parker.** You'll also find a nice selection of upscale clothing shops.

SID AND ANN MASHBURN
1198 Howell Mill Rd., 404-350-7132
www.annmashburn.com
www.sidmashburn.com
NEIGHBORHOOD: <u>Westside Urban Market</u> (next to the Westside Provisions District)
Sid and Ann share the same location, but offer different lines. The men's clothing shop offers everything from socks to suits. The women's shop boasts a classic approach to dressing a woman offering everything from blouses and dresses to jewelry, shirtdresses, pencil & wrap skirts.

SWEET AUBURN CURB MARKET
209 Edgewood Ave SE, Atlanta, 404-659-1665
www.thecurbmarket.com
NEIGHBORHOOD: Downtown
"USA Today" ranked this place as the 16th best food market in the world. It houses 24 independently-owned businesses from eateries to retail shops. There are plenty of places to eat fried chicken in Atlanta, so maybe you should skip the excellent chicken at the **Metro Deli Soul Food** hot bar, and opt instead for something a little different like Venezuelan arepas or the really nice and spicy Jamaican meat patties. One of my favorites is **Panbury's Double Crust Pies**, where the South African owners have adapted the pie concept so popular in

their homeland to Atlanta, which explains why I like their Southern Breakfast Pie so much (with eggs, chicken sausage, and maple syrup). Other standouts are their Cajun Chicken Gumbo Pie with chicken, Andouille sausage, and Cajun spices, and the Cracked-Black-Pepper Steak Pie made with slow-braised beef shoulder and gravy. **Grindhouse Killer Burgers**, which has a couple of other locations in Atlanta, is here, too.

UNDERGROUND ATLANTA
www.underground-atlanta.com/
50 Upper Alabama St., 404-523-2311
Customer service center, 404-523-2311 ext. 7019
NEIGHBORHOOD: Downtown
Whether you want to shop, go to a bar, enjoy some varied nightlife or want to go eat, Underground Atlanta is a place where you can do it all. This popular tourist attraction is literally underground and is close to other

downtown attractions such as the **World of Coca-Cola** and the **Georgia Aquarium**. Tour and local attraction tickets are available for purchase at several kiosks in the Underground, as well as shopping at a variety of unique retail stores. Located in the heart of the downtown, Underground Atlanta is one of the city's favorite attractions and a cultural hub. Opened in 1969 as a "city beneath the streets," Underground Atlanta still exhibits many of the significant architectural features from its original structure. Visitors can pick up a self-guided history tour brochure at the information booth and discover the history firsthand. Explore six city blocks, 12 acres and three levels of 225,000 square feet of shopping, restaurants and entertainment at Underground Atlanta, a destination with more than 100 years of history.

VINO VENUE
4478 Chamblee Dunwoody Rd., 770) 668-0435
www.atlantawineschool.com/
Want to learn more about wine? Here's the place, but

if you're just visiting, stop by this 4,000 square foot emporium to taste from among 50 bottles. Wine bar, food items as well as shopping.

WESTSIDE PROVISIONS DISTRICT
1100 Howell Mill Rd. NW, 404-872-7538
www.westsidepd.com
NEIGHBORHOOD: West Midtown
The district is a center of shopping and dining with a variety of retail boutiques and award-winning restaurants. Restaurants include: Bacchanalia, West Egg Café, Taqueria del Sol, JCT. Kitchen & Bar, and Ormsby's. Shopping spots include Star Provisions, a gourmet shop.

Index

Y

Other Books by the Same Author

Andrew Delaplaine has written in widely varied fields: screenplays, novels (adult and juvenile), travel writing, journalism. His books are available in quality bookstores as well as all online retailers.

JACK HOUSTON / ST. CLAIR POLITICAL THRILLERS

THE KEYSTONE FILE – PART 1
THE KEYSTONE FILE – PART 2
THE KEYSTONE FILE – PART 3
THE KEYSTONE FILE – PART 4
THE KEYSTONE FILE – PART 5
THE KEYSTONE FILE – PART 6
THE KEYSTONE FILE – PART 7 *(FINAL)*

On Election night, as China and Russia mass soldiers on their common border in preparation for war, there's a tie in the Electoral College that forces the decision for President into the House of Representatives as mandated by the Constitution. The incumbent Republican President, working through his Aide for Congressional Liaison, uses the Keystone File, which contains dirt on every member of Congress, to blackmail members into supporting the Republican candidate. The action runs from Election Night in November to Inauguration Day on January 20. Jack Houston St. Clair runs a small detective agency in Miami. His father is Florida Governor Sam Houston St. Clair, the Republican candidate. While he tries to help his dad win the election, Jack also gets hired to follow up on some suspicious wire transfers involving drug smugglers, leading him to a sunken narco-sub off Key West that has $65 million in cash in its hull.

THE RUNNING MATE

Sam Houston St. Clair has been President for four long years and right now he's bogged down in a nasty fight to be re-elected. A Secret Service agent protecting the opposing candidate discovers that the candidate is sleeping with someone he shouldn't be, and tells his lifelong friend, the President's son Jack, this vital information so Jack can pass it on to help his father win the election. The candidate's wife has also found out about the clandestine affair and plots to kill the lover if her husband wins the election. Jack goes to Washington, and becomes involved in an international whirlpool of intrigue.

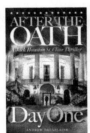 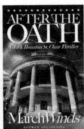 

AFTER THE OATH: DAY ONE
AFTER THE OATH: MARCH WINDS
WEDDING AT THE WHITE HOUSE

Only three months have passed since Sam Houston St. Clair was sworn in as the new President, but a lot has happened. Returning from Vienna where he met with Russian and Chinese diplomats, Sam is making his way back to Flagler Hall in Miami, his first trip home since being inaugurated. Son Jack is in the midst of turmoil of his own back in Miami, dealing with various dramas, not the least of which is his increasing alienation from Babylon Fuentes and his growing attraction to the seductive Lupe Rodriguez. Fernando Pozo addresses new problems as he struggles to expand Cuba's secret operations in the U.S., made even more difficult as U.S.-Cuban relations thaw. As his father returns home, Jack knows Sam will find as much trouble at home as he did in Vienna.

THE ADVENTURES OF SHERLOCK HOLMES IV

In this series, the original Sherlock Holmes's great-great-great grandson solves crimes and mysteries in the present day, working out of the boutique hotel he owns on South Beach.

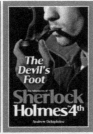

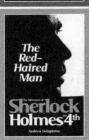

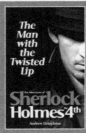

THE BOSCOMBE VALLEY MYSTERY

Sherlock Holmes and Watson are called to a remote area of Florida overlooking Lake Okeechobee to investigate a murder where all the evidence points to the victim's son as the killer. Holmes, however, is not so sure.

THE DEVIL'S FOOT

Holmes's doctor orders him to take a short holiday in Key West, and while there, Holmes is called on to look into a case in which three people involved in a Santería ritual died with no explanation.

THE CLEVER ONE

A former nun who, while still very devout, has renounced her vows so that she could "find a life, and possibly love, in the real world." She comes to Holmes in hopes that he can find out what happened to the man who promised to marry her, but mysteriously disappeared moments before their wedding.

THE COPPER BEECHES

A nanny reaches out to Sherlock Holmes seeking his advice on whether she should take a new position when her prospective employer has demanded that she cut her hair as part of the job.

THE RED-HAIRED MAN

A man with a shock of red hair calls on Sherlock Holmes to solve the mystery of the Red-haired League.

THE SIX NAPOLEONS

Inspector Lestrade calls on Holmes to help him figure out why a madman would go around Miami breaking into homes and businesses to destroy cheap busts of the French Emperor. It all seems very insignificant to Holmes—until, of course, a murder occurs.

THE MAN WITH THE TWISTED LIP

In what seems to be the case of a missing person, Sherlock Holmes navigates his way through a maze of perplexing clues that leads him through a sinister world to a surprising conclusion.

THE BORNHOLM DIAMOND

A mysterious Swedish nobleman requests a meeting to discuss a matter of such serious importance that it may threaten the line of succession in one of the oldest royal houses in Europe.

SEVERAL TITLES IN THE DELAPLAINE SERIES OF PRE-SCHOOL READERS FOR CHILDREN

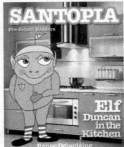

THE DELAPLAINE LONG WEEKEND TRAVEL GUIDE SERIES

Delaplaine Travel Guides represent the author's take on some of the many cities he's visited and many of which he has called home (for months or even years) during a lifetime of travel. The books are available as either ebooks or as printed books. Owing to the ease with which material can be uploaded, both the printed and ebook editions are updated 3 times a year.

Annapolis

Appalachicola

Atlanta

Austin

Berlin

Beverly Hills

Birmingham

Boston

Brooklyn

Cancún (Mexico)

Cannes

Cape Cod

Charleston

Charlotte

Chicago

Clearwater – St. Petersburg

Coral Gables

El Paso

Fort Lauderdale

Fort Myers & Sanibel

Gettysburg

Hilton Head

Hood River (Ore.)

Jacksonville

Key West & the Florida Keys

Las Vegas

London

Los Angeles / Downtown

Louisville

Marseille

Martha's Vineyard

Memphis

Mérida (Mexico)

Mexico City

Miami & South Beach

Milwaukee

Myrtle Beach

Nantucket

Napa Valley

Naples & Marco Island

Nashville

New Orleans

New York / The Bronx

New York / Downtown

New York / Midtown

New York / Queens

New York / Upper East Side

New York / Upper West Side

Orlando & the Theme Parks

Palm Beach

Panama City (Fla.)

Paris

Pensacola

Philadelphia

Portland (Ore.)

Provincetown

Rio de Janeiro

San Francisco

San Juan

Santa Monica & Venice

Sarasota

Savannah

Seattle

Sonoma County

Tampa Bay

Washington, D.C.

West Hollywood & Hollywood

THE FOOD ENTHUSIAST'S
COMPLETE RESTAURANT GUIDES

CPSIA information can be obtained
at www.ICGtesting.com
Printed in the USA
BVHW03s1145150518
516306BV00010B/63/P